P9-BHR-350

LET'S EXPLORE LIFE SCIENCE

Exploring

ECOSYSTEMS

Ella Hawley

PowerKiDS
press.

New York

Published in 2013 by The Rosen Publishing Group, Inc.
29 East 21st Street, New York, NY 10010

First Edition

Editor: Jennifer Way
Book Design: Kate Laczynski

Photo Credits: Cover (main image, fish, mouse), pp. 4, 5, 6, 7, 10 (all images), 11 (all images), 12, 13 (left, right), 14, 15, 16, 17 (left, right), 18, 20, 21 (left, right), 22 Shutterstock.com; pp. 8–9 © www.iStockphoto.com/John Anderson; p. 19 iStockphoto/Thinkstock.

Library of Congress Cataloging-in-Publication Data

Hawley, Ella.
 Exploring ecosystems / by Ella Hawley. — 1st ed.
     p. cm. — (Let's explore life science)
 Includes index.
 ISBN 978-1-4488-6175-0 (library binding) — ISBN 978-1-4488-6314-3 (pbk.) — ISBN 978-1-4488-6307-5 (6-pack)
 1. Biotic communities—Juvenile literature. I. Title.
 QH541.14.H388 2013
 577—dc23
                                                              2011025275

Manufactured in the United States of America

CPSIA Compliance Information: Batch #SW12PK: For Further Information contact Rosen Publishing, New York, New York at 1-800-237-9932

CONTENTS

What Are Ecosystems?

Do you know what an ecosystem is? You do not have to go far to find one. You can just open your door and step outside. Your backyard and even the cracks in the sidewalk are ecosystems. Anywhere that plants and animals are interacting with each other and their surroundings is an ecosystem.

A pond ecosystem is made up of the plants, animals, soil, and water in and around the pond. The flowers shown growing in this pond are lotuses.

Frogs hunt for insects in pond ecosystems.

Ecosystems can be made up of many different habitats or just one. They can also be as big as a whole **biome**, such as a desert, or as small as a pond or a puddle.

Parts of an Ecosystem

Plants need the nutrients and water found in soil to live.

Living things count on other living things in their ecosystem. They also count on nonliving things. Air, light and heat from the Sun, water, rocks, and all the nonliving things that make up our world are important parts of ecosystems.

Plants use light from the Sun to make food. They take in carbon dioxide from the air and put out

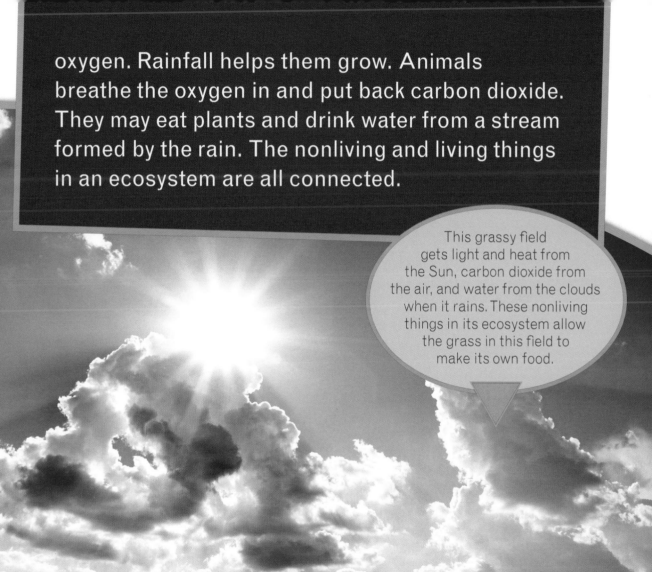

oxygen. Rainfall helps them grow. Animals breathe the oxygen in and put back carbon dioxide. They may eat plants and drink water from a stream formed by the rain. The nonliving and living things in an ecosystem are all connected.

This grassy field gets light and heat from the Sun, carbon dioxide from the air, and water from the clouds when it rains. These nonliving things in its ecosystem allow the grass in this field to make its own food.

Biodiversity and Balance

Biodiversity is a measure of how many different kinds of living things live in an ecosystem. Generally, healthy ecosystems are home to many different kinds of living things.

Herbivores, or plant eaters, feed on the plants in an ecosystem. Herbivores help new plants grow by spreading seeds. If there are lots of different kinds of herbivores in an ecosystem, then meat eaters will have lots of **prey**. The meat

Coral is a tiny marine animal that lives in colonies in warm, shallow ocean waters. These colonies form coral reefs, shown here. Fish, sea sponges, shrimp, crabs, jellyfish, and sharks are just a few of the living things in a coral-reef ecosystem.

eaters help keep the numbers of plant eaters down so they do not eat too many plants at once. All the parts of an ecosystem work together to keep nature in balance.

Food Chains and Food Webs

ROLES IN THE FOOD CHAIN

	PRODUCER	PRIMARY CONSUMER	SECONDARY CONSUMER
Food Source	Makes its own food	Eats plants	Eats plants and animals or only animals
Also Known As	Plants	Herbivores	Omnivores or Carnivores
Example	Grass	Grasshopper	Mouse

Life in an ecosystem involves give and take. This relationship between living organisms is called the food chain. Many connected food chains are called food webs.

Every food chain and food web starts with plants. Plants are called producers because they make their own food using energy from the Sun. Plant-eating

TERTIARY CONSUMER	QUATERNARY CONSUMER	SCAVENGER	DECOMPOSER
Eats animals	Eats animals	Eats dead animals	Breaks down dead plant or animal matter
Carnivores	Carnivores	Scavengers	Decomposers
Snake	Owl	Vulture	Mushrooms

animals eat the plants. Then meat-eating animals eat those animals. Some animals eat both plants and animals. All of these animals are called **consumers**. The last group in a food chain is the **decomposers**. Decomposers break down dead plant and animal matter. This returns nutrients to the soil and helps plants grow.

A Look at a Desert Ecosystem

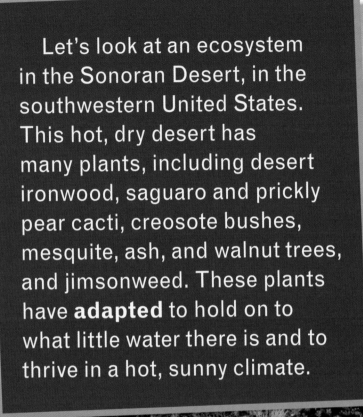

Let's look at an ecosystem in the Sonoran Desert, in the southwestern United States. This hot, dry desert has many plants, including desert ironwood, saguaro and prickly pear cacti, creosote bushes, mesquite, ash, and walnut trees, and jimsonweed. These plants have **adapted** to hold on to what little water there is and to thrive in a hot, sunny climate.

Cacti in the Sonoran Desert are adapted to soak up any rain that falls and use that water slowly.

The animals that live in the Sonoran Desert include jackrabbits, mountain lions, Gila monsters, toads, owls, and rattlesnakes. Many of these animals find shady spots to rest in during the day. Then they come out to look for food at night, when it is cooler.

Jackrabbits are primary consumers that eat desert grasses and shrubs. They make their nests in the shrubby undergrowth of plants such as sagebrush.

Gila monsters are secondary consumers that live in underground burrows that are nice and cool during hot desert days. These lizards eat mostly bird and reptile eggs.

A Look at a Grassland Ecosystem

The Serengeti is an ecosystem in the African countries of Tanzania and Kenya. Much of it is savanna. Here a group of zebras have gathered by a watering hole near an acacia tree.

Some plants and animals live in grassland ecosystems. Tropical grasslands, such as those in Africa, are called savannas.

Many plants and animals make their home on the African savanna. Zebras, gazelles, and water buffalo graze on grasses. Giraffes munch leaves from the few trees there. Lions and cheetahs hunt these animals. As plants and animals die, decomposers such as fungi, worms, insects, and bacteria get to work breaking the matter down. This puts nutrients back into the soil so more grasses can grow. All these plants and animals need each other to keep the ecosystem healthy.

Cheetahs are carnivores that live in the Serengeti. They hunt primary consumers like zebras.

A Walk in a Tropical Rain Forest

The Amazon rain forest is one of the world's best-known rain forests. There are also tropical rain forests in Asia, Australia, and Africa.

Warm, wet tropical rain forests are one of the world's most biodiverse ecosystems. The Amazon rain forest, in South America, has the greatest number of **species** of plants and animals in the world. Rain forests have lots of tall trees. Vines grow up the tree trunks. Ferns and many other plants grow in the shade below the trees.

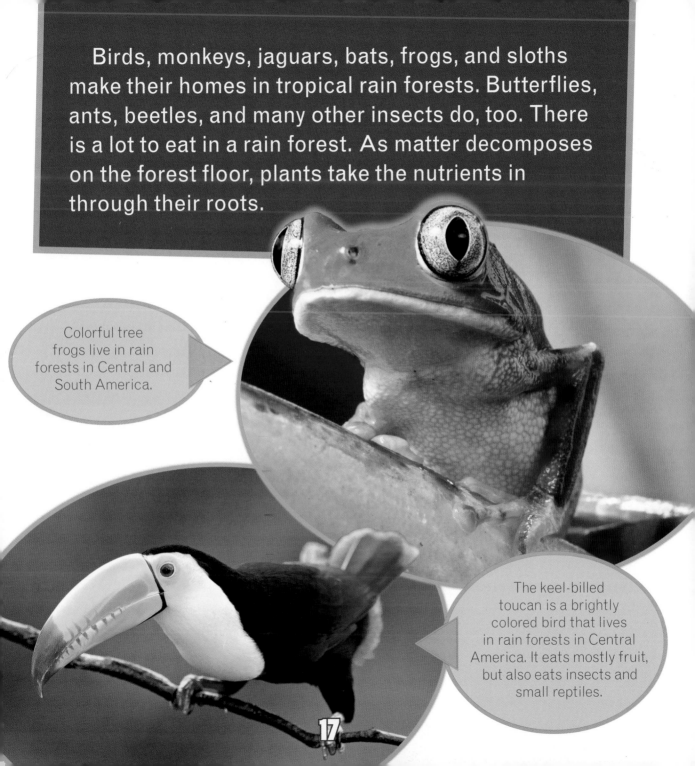

Birds, monkeys, jaguars, bats, frogs, and sloths make their homes in tropical rain forests. Butterflies, ants, beetles, and many other insects do, too. There is a lot to eat in a rain forest. As matter decomposes on the forest floor, plants take the nutrients in through their roots.

Colorful tree frogs live in rain forests in Central and South America.

The keel-billed toucan is a brightly colored bird that lives in rain forests in Central America. It eats mostly fruit, but also eats insects and small reptiles.

Other Forest Ecosystems

Deciduous forests can be found in eastern North America, Europe, eastern Asia, Australia, New Zealand, and on the southern tip of South America.

Rain forests are not the only forest ecosystems. There are also **deciduous** and **coniferous** forests. Deciduous forests have trees that lose their leaves in the winter. Deciduous forests have trees, shrubs, ferns, mosses, and lichens. Squirrels, raccoons, deer, wolves, birds, bats, and insects are just a few of the animals that live in these forests.

Coniferous forests are made up mainly of evergreen trees, or fir trees. They grow in places that have long, cold winters and wet summers. Shrubs, plants, fungi, mosses, and lichens grow beneath the trees. Birds, insects, shrews, weasels, moose, and reindeer live in coniferous forests.

Squirrels live in deciduous forests. They have a role in their ecosystem that you might not know about. Squirrels bury food to save it for later. Sometimes they do not dig this food up. If that lost food was an acorn, it can grow into a new tree!

The Treeless Tundra

The ecosystem with the least biodiversity is the tundra. The tundra is very cold and no trees grow there. Even in the warmest season, only the top of the soil melts. Beneath that, the ground stays frozen all year. This is called permafrost.

Many kinds of shrubs, lichens, and grasses grow there. Animals such as caribou and arctic hares eat

Tundra vegetation includes low shrubs, grasses, mosses, and lichens.

the plants and lichen. Arctic foxes, wolves, and polar bears hunt these animals for food. Many birds and insects also come to the tundra when it is warmer. Some animals have adapted by **migrating** during the coldest weather.

Wolverines live in the tundra of North America, Asia, and Europe.

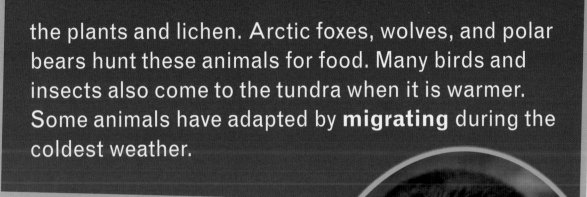

Caribou live in the tundra in North America, Scandinavia, Northern China, and Russia. These herbivores migrate to the southern part of their range in winter and move back north when the weather gets warmer.

Saving Earth's Ecosystems

Some of Earth's ecosystems are in trouble. As people clear land to build houses, farms, roads, and businesses, there is less space for plants and animals to live. People **pollute** the air and are causing problems like **global climate change**. This upsets nature's balance.

Denali National Park and Preserve is in Alaska. A national preserve is a protected ecosystem where hunting, building homes, and drilling for oil or gas are not allowed.

The good news is we can help keep Earth's ecosystems healthy. We can protect wilderness areas and the plants and animals that live there. We can reuse and recycle things that would end up in landfills or dirty our land and water. These actions all help keep Earth's ecosystems safe. What will you do to help?

22

GLOSSARY

adapted (uh-DAPT-ed) Changed to fit new conditions.

biodiversity (by-oh-dih-VER-sih-tee) The number of different types of living things that are found in a certain place on Earth.

biome (BY-ohm) A kind of place with certain weather patterns and kinds of plants.

coniferous (kah-NIH-fur-us) Having cones and needlelike leaves.

consumers (kun-SOO-merz) Members of the food chain that eat other living things.

deciduous (deh-SIH-joo-us) Having leaves that fall off every year.

decomposers (dee-kum-POH-zerz) Living things that break down the cells of dead plants and animals into simpler parts.

global climate change (GLOH-bul KLY-mut CHAYNG) A slow increase in how hot Earth is. It is caused by gases that are let out when people burn fuels such as gasoline.

herbivores (ER-buh-vorz) Animals that eat only plants.

migrating (MY-grayt-ing) Moving from one place to another.

pollute (puh-LOOT) To poison with harmful matter.

prey (PRAY) An animal that is hunted by another animal for food.

species (SPEE-sheez) One kind of living thing. All people are one species.

INDEX

WEB SITES

Due to the changing nature of Internet links, PowerKids Press has developed an online list of Web sites related to the subject of this book. This site is updated regularly. Please use this link to access the list:
www.powerkidslinks.com/lels/eco/

24